I0795390

IMAGES
of America

Miami's Brickell Avenue Neighborhood

On the Cover: This photograph, taken in 1928, captures the youth and innocence of the girls who attended the Miss Harris Florida School in the heart of the Brickell Avenue neighborhood. This educational institution was an important part of Miami from 1922 until it moved north in 1957. (Courtesy of State of Florida Archives.)

IMAGES
of America

MIAMI'S BRICKELL AVENUE NEIGHBORHOOD

Paul S. George and Casey Piket

ARCADIA
PUBLISHING

ISBN 978-1-4671-0518-7

Published by Arcadia Publishing
Charleston, South Carolina

Printed in the United States of America

Library of Congress Control Number: 2020931558

For all general information, please contact Arcadia Publishing:
Telephone 843-853-2070
Fax 843-853-0044
E-mail sales@arcadiapublishing.com
For customer service and orders:
Toll-Free 1-888-313-2665

Visit us on the Internet at www.arcadiapublishing.com

Dr. Paul George would like to dedicate this book to and thank his family—wife Laura, daughter Maryrose, and sons Paul Jr. and Matthew—for their infinite patience and support during this project.

Casey M. Piket would like to dedicate this book to his father and late mother, both of whom were born and raised in the Magic City, for the inspiration to research and a write a book about a city that five generations of family members have called home.

Contents

ACKNOWLEDGMENTS

The Brickell Avenue neighborhood is one of the most dynamic quarters in the eastern United States. Bustling with a rich street life amid a forest of glistening high-rise residential palaces, the neighborhood resonates with activity throughout the day and night, a remarkable departure from the quiet of just 30 years ago.

Oddly, the neighborhood has not been the subject of a major historical undertaking until now. This book examines the rich history and meteoric rise of the neighborhood through the medium of photographs, providing an overview of the neighborhood's evolution in the last 150 years. Readers will see and experience the development of a gorgeous subtropical hammock into a picturesque neighborhood of single-family homes and tourist accommodations. Both yielded in recent years to a rising banking and financial center and, more recently, the stunning residential, retail, and restaurant district of today.

Both authors have written extensively of the Brickell Avenue neighborhood. Both provide detailed historical, architectural, and archaeological tours of the neighborhood. Both lecture on its rich history and have created podcasts to share its story to listeners near and far. With this background and the knowledge accrued from these forays into history, we felt that Brickell's time to be showcased in a historical manner was now.

There are many people who deserve credit for the completion of this book. The folks at the Research Center at HistoryMiami Museum, including Ashley Trujillo, Michelle Avalos, and Jeremy Salloum, were invaluable in the discovery and imaging of some of the photographs in this book. A special thank-you to historian Larry Wiggins, Laura Hemphill, and Saint Rosemund for sharing and allowing the use of photographs from their personal collections. Also, thank you to Eileen Lehn for providing editorial services for parts of the book, and to Caroline Anderson, our project manager with Arcadia Publishing, for providing guidance as we navigated the process to complete this publication.

We hope readers of *Miami's Brickell Avenue Neighborhood* will enjoy and learn from this book while coming to understand that the evolution of this part of Miami from "just yesterday" has been stunning, unique, and unlike any other district in a major American city. Thank you to all who have purchased and enjoyed this publication!

INTRODUCTION

Miami's Brickell Avenue has evolved in 150 years from a subtropical wilderness studded with tall oak trees and an impassable underbrush to its present status as southeast Florida's most exciting neighborhood. In 1871, the large Brickell family, headed by William and Mary, entered this desolate Eden bracketed by the Miami River and Biscayne Bay, and instituted its slow transformation, first opening what became a busy trading post while methodically acquiring thousands of acres through purchase and federal homestead laws.

Born in Ohio, William Brickell was stricken by wanderlust and an entrepreneurial spirit, visiting California at a young age during its mid-century gold rush, and later Australia during its own gold strike in the 1860s. There he met young Mary Bulmer, who, along with her family, had migrated from England. The couple married in the late 1860s and moved to the United States. Soon they set out for another frontier, the wilds of southeast Florida.

The family's vast real estate holdings remained undeveloped until Henry M. Flagler's Florida East Coast Railway steamed into Miami in April 1896. Thereafter, the Brickells began to sell, lease, develop, and rent portions of their properties along today's Brickell Avenue and points east. What began to emerge was a tranquil neighborhood of wood frame homes with open porches and pitched roofs by the bay and the river. By the 1920s, more grand homes began to appear. The southern portions of Brickell Avenue became a "Millionaire Row" after Mary Brickell sold large lots backing to the warm waters of Biscayne Bay. Grand homes in the Beaux-Arts and Mediterranean styles became winter homes for prominent families from the northeastern United States.

The Great Depression caused some homeowners to subdivide their residences into rooming houses. The period following World War II brought additional changes as small numbers of retail and institutional buildings appeared on Brickell Avenue. By the late 1970s, the old Millionaire Row was giving way to tall condominiums with avant-garde designs. The era of Brickell skyscrapers was under way. In the meantime, Brickell was on the road to becoming a financial center hosting offices of banks with headquarters in many corners of the world.

By the beginning of the new century, nearly all of the neighborhood's original housing stock was gone and the first of two booms that would transform Brickell into the "Manhattan of South Florida" had begun. With its forest of high-rises, including two of the tallest buildings in the southeastern United States, the Brickell Avenue neighborhood has become an entertainment and residential paradise second to none in the region.

One

Brickell Point

The prospering Brickell family built their large, beautiful Neoclassical home on the site of today's Icon Brickell complex, near Brickell Avenue and Southeast Fifth Street, in the 1900s. In this 1906 photograph, William Brickell is seated in the center on the ground-floor porch. Standing around and above him are several of his and Mary's children. The home stood until the mid-1960s. (Courtesy of HistoryMiami Museum.)

William Brickell, seen here as a young man, was born in Steubenville, Ohio, in 1835. An adventurous sort with a streak of entrepreneurship, he traveled widely. He was in California at the time of the Gold Rush in the late 1840s and spent several years in Australia during its own gold rush in the mid-1800s, operating a large hotel, coach service, and grocery store. There, he met Mary Bulmer, a young Englishwoman who had migrated to the remote continent with her family. They married in 1862 and soon after sailed to the United States. After many years in Ohio, the restive William Brickell sailed to the remote Miami area, arriving on New Year's Day 1871. With him was Ephraim Sturtevant, whose daughter Julia Tuttle is considered the "Mother of Miami." The rest of the family joined Brickell later that year. They operated an Indian trading post on the south bank of the Miami River while accumulating a vast amount of land near their home and elsewhere. (Courtesy of HistoryMiami Museum.)

Mary Brickell presents a severe look in this photograph. Although she was all business when it came to the family's holdings, Mary was generous with loans and in other ways. She was also astute with real estate and likely exerted a stronger influence over the family properties than her husband, who could be difficult in his dealings with people. Mary oversaw the construction of a trail through the thick hammock where the family lived. The trail was meant to link their trading post on the Miami River with the flourishing community of Coconut Grove, several miles south. From this pathway would emerge Brickell Avenue. Mary was also responsible for the later widening and beautification of the street. Today, Brickell Avenue is one of the most attractive, important, and flourishing thoroughfares in Florida. A small bust of her sits in the northern portion of the median as a later generation has embraced her as a visionary and critical element in the development of early Miami. (Courtesy of HistoryMiami Museum.)

In this close-up view of the image on page 9, William Brickell is surrounded by sons, other intimates, and a dog in front of the family home, built a few years earlier. Brickell had just three more years of life left, but could look back on a lifetime of travel and success that few of his contemporaries could claim. (Courtesy of HistoryMiami Museum.)

This 1898 photograph of Brickell Point at the mouth of the Miami River looks south over the small complex of the Brickells' Indian trading post along with other structures developed by the family in the wooded area beyond. At this time, the Brickells were already seeing a steep rise in the value of their property. (Courtesy of State Library and Archives of Florida.)

This view of the young city dates to the early 1900s. In contrast to the south bank of the Miami River, the north bank, hosting downtown as well as Flagler's magnificent Royal Palm Hotel, was filled with activity. Brickell Point and the beginnings of a neighborhood known as Southside, which corresponds to today's Brickell Avenue neighborhood, can be seen at left. (Courtesy of HistoryMiami Museum.)

This early-1900s aerial view of the Miami River shows, at left, the different levels of development of the Brickell Avenue neighborhood, then known as Southside. The trees in the foreground gave way to boatyards and other maritime businesses beyond the Miami Avenue Bridge. (Courtesy of HistoryMiami Museum.)

This 1900 photograph contrasts the rapidly developing north bank of the Miami River with Henry Flagler's magnificent Royal Palm Hotel in the distance and the rustic Brickell property with its sandy pathway flanked by coconut palms on the south bank. Development of the Brickell properties was still several years away. (Casey M. Piket.)

This postcard, created from a photograph in 1918, indicates how primeval portions of the Brickell Avenue neighborhood remained more than 20 years after the incorporation of the City of Miami and the commencement of development. The Brickells methodically developed their properties near the river, building handsome homes and planting attractive trees, such as the coconut palms lining this pathway. (Casey M. Piket.)

This photograph illustrates the Brickells' efforts to develop their properties after the arrival of Henry M. Flagler's Florida East Coast Railway to Miami in 1896. The Brickells built several homes they later leased to prominent families who were awaiting completion of their own residences. One of the homes pictured, at 401 Brickell Avenue, was rented to millionaire industrialist James Deering from 1914 through 1916 while his home Vizcaya was being constructed. It was later rented to Charles Deering, James's brother and head of the giant International Harvester Corporation, while his estate was under construction in south Dade County. The foliage around the two buildings harkened back to the raw frontier that was the Brickell property only a few years earlier. (Courtesy of HistoryMiami Museum.)

This colorful painting of Charles Deering seated at Brickell Point was the work of John Singer Sargent, one of America's preeminent artists and portrait painters. The erudite and cultured Deering, who had served as chairman of the board of the family's International Harvester Corporation, was a Miami mainstay by the mid-1910s and was involved in building his namesake estate in deep south Dade County. (Casey M. Piket.)

Miami was a subtropical paradise in its early decades. One reason for the city's beauty was the plethora of coconut palm trees that studded the banks of the Miami River. At the top of this photograph, taken in the early 1920s, Brickell Point is blessed with plenty of coconut palms, obscuring the view of the early homes there. (Casey M. Piket.)

The great real estate boom of the mid-1920s transformed Miami from a young, frontier community to an emerging metropolitan area. This aerial view of the mouth of the river, taken in 1925 by Richard B. Hoit, a prolific early Miami photographer, underlines the undeveloped nature of the Brickell Avenue area on the left in contrast to the north bank and other parts of Miami, which underwent a dramatic transformation. One reason for the Brickell area's paucity of development was the lack of a bridge connecting the neighborhood with the city's bustling downtown. The Brickell Avenue Bridge would not appear until 1930, and even with the direct connection it afforded, the Brickell Avenue neighborhood remained a quiet district of single-family homes and apartments with a small retail sector along South Miami Avenue. (Courtesy of Miami-Dade Public Library, Romer Collection.)

This 1927 photograph from Brickell Point gives a rare view of Henry M. Flagler's magnificent Royal Palm Hotel on the north side of the river. Thirty years after its opening, the hotel looks fit and attractive. However, it closed its doors soon after and was razed in 1930. Miami's first luxury hotel, the Royal Palm was a winter home for the Carnegies, Vanderbilts, and Rockefellers, among others. (Courtesy of Miami-Dade Public Library, Romer Collection.)

Brickell Point is in the foreground on the south bank of the Miami River. In this 1928 photograph, the edge of Brickell Point remained undeveloped, while the north bank of the river featured the prominent Fort Dallas Park residential neighborhood. Later, Fort Dallas Park transitioned from single-family residences to mid-rise apartment buildings and hotels, as seen here. (Courtesy of Miami-Dade Public Library, Romer Collection.)

By the 1930s, Miami was already an important commercial airline center. The three Pan Am Clippers seen in this 1934 photograph are flying high above the Brickell Avenue neighborhood, much of which continued to host dense stands of trees while its grand era of development still lay ahead. It is likely the Clippers were returning to Pan Am's Dinner Key airport. (Courtesy of Miami-Dade Public Library, Romer Collection.)

Mary Brickell and her youngest child, Maude, are seen in this 1921 photograph at their home on Brickell Point. Mary was then 84 years old, with less than a year of life left. The determination and steely reserve that characterized her demeanor are evident. (Courtesy of HistoryMiami Museum.)

This 1950s photograph, taken from Brickell Point, shows the gaping hole across the Miami River where the Royal Palm Hotel once stood. Following the demolition of the hotel in 1930, the site hosted large parking lots immediately southeast of downtown. (Casey M. Piket.)

For many years, the Miami River has played a central role in the history of Miami. This view shows its mouth in 1951. On the right, or south, is the Brickell Avenue area with its warehouses and boatyards. This bustling river is today the fifth busiest port in the state of Florida. (Courtesy of Miami-Dade Public Library, Romer Collection.)

By the mid-20th century, the proud Brickell mansion, by now 50 years of age, was not only exhibiting the wear and tear of time, but also a hint of abandonment since its lone occupant by then was Maude Brickell, the youngest child of William and Mary Brickell. The neighborhood around it was developing in the early postwar flush of prosperity as a beautiful residential enclave with a dash of retail across Brickell Avenue from the home and the beautiful First Presbyterian Church to the south. This photograph was taken on August 26, 1954. The home was razed in January 1961. (Courtesy of HistoryMiami Museum.)

Brickell family members were buried in a splendid garden cemetery bedecked with flowering plants. In the 1920s, the family built a Neoclassical-style mausoleum near the original graveyard. It served the Brickells until the late 1940s, when the remains were removed to a mausoleum in Miami's Woodlawn Park Cemetery. The earlier mausoleum remains on its original site in what became Brickell Park in the 1920s. (Courtesy of HistoryMiami Museum.)

Built in the 1920s, the Brickell mausoleum contained the remains of Brickell family members until they were moved to the Woodlawn Park Cemetery in the late 1940s. This photograph was taken shortly before the home, seen in the background, was razed. The mausoleum remains in Brickell Park. (Courtesy of HistoryMiami Museum.)

This 1982 view, looking from north to south, provides a different aspect of the Brickell Avenue area. Visible are the Brickell Point Apartments, the new Holiday Inn Hotel towering over them, the bridge connecting the mainland to Claughton Island, and the imposing Four Ambassadors, which arose just south of the bridge in the late 1960s. (Courtesy of HistoryMiami Museum.)

These photographs show the Brickell Point Apartments in February 1989. Built in 1950 on the edge of the river on Brickell Point, the apartment complex was beginning to show its age. Behind the apartments was the Sheraton Hotel, built as a Holiday Inn in 1980. Both the hotel and apartment buildings were constructed on the former site of the Brickell family home and trading post. The area was referred to as Brickell Point until the discovery of the Tequesta circle in 1998. The apartments advertised the opportunity to live within walking distance of downtown, which offered residents who worked in an office building in the city a very short commute. (Both, Dr. Paul S. George.)

The Brickell Point Apartments at the mouth of the Miami River are seen here in the months immediately before their demolition. By then, this complex, which stirred excitement upon its completion in 1950, was in poor shape from years of neglect. Developer Michael Bauman purchased the property for $8.5 million with plans to develop two condominium towers there. That plan was waylaid after archaeologists uncovered the famed Miami Circle in 1998, which was a circular carving in the bedrock a couple feet beneath the surface. After international press coverage and an outcry from the public, the county and state collaborated on the purchase of the site from Bauman for $26.7 million. Artifacts found in the circle were dated at more than 2,000 years old. (Courtesy of HistoryMiami Museum.)

The Miami Circle is one of the most famous archaeological discoveries in recent decades. A perfectly circular carving in the limestone, it is 38 feet in diameter with the carved elements within it resembling the spokes of a giant wheel. Postholes pock the circle's perimeter; presumably, they held logs buttressing a wall, roof, or both. The structure sits on Brickell Point and was unknown until its discovery at the end of the 20th century. Under strong pressure from an energized public, the State of Florida and Miami-Dade County purchased the two-acre site bracketing the circle for $26.7 million. The space serves as a park with the circle at its center. The circle's dedication, seen here, took place in February 2011. Its preservation ranks with the most outstanding achievements in this field. (Casey M. Piket.)

Two

Brickell Key on Claughton Island

This is an aerial view of Burlingame Island in 1916. It was named for Margaret and John Burlingame, who were awarded the spoil island by the Florida Improvement Fund in 1912 after they outbid Mary Brickell. The island was created as a result of the sediment from dredging near the mouth of the Miami River and farther west in the Everglades. (Courtesy of Miami-Dade Public Library, Romer Collection.)

Burlingame Island is pictured in 1935. At this time, the island was nearly 21 acres following a dredge and fill campaign by R.P. Clark, who purchased it in 1932. Across from the island until 1930, on the north side of the mouth of the Miami River, was Flagler's Royal Palm Hotel. (Courtesy of HistoryMiami Museum.)

Here is another view of an expanded Burlingame Island in 1935. By then, the island was filled and bulkheaded into its familiar triangular shape. Australian pine trees began to appear on parts of the island, which provided a semblance of green space on the otherwise barren land. (Courtesy of State Library and Archives of Florida.)

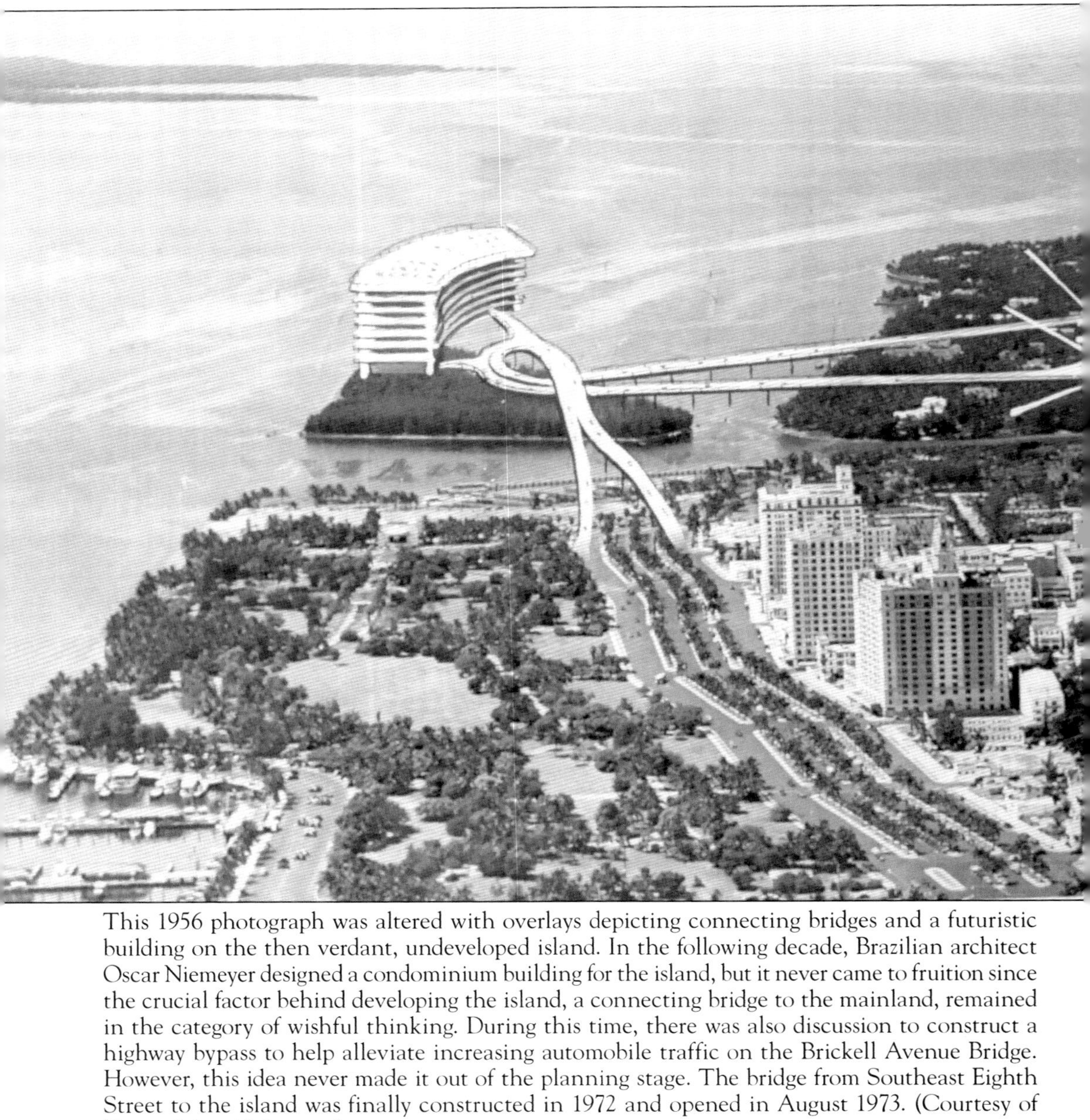

This 1956 photograph was altered with overlays depicting connecting bridges and a futuristic building on the then verdant, undeveloped island. In the following decade, Brazilian architect Oscar Niemeyer designed a condominium building for the island, but it never came to fruition since the crucial factor behind developing the island, a connecting bridge to the mainland, remained in the category of wishful thinking. During this time, there was also discussion to construct a highway bypass to help alleviate increasing automobile traffic on the Brickell Avenue Bridge. However, this idea never made it out of the planning stage. The bridge from Southeast Eighth Street to the island was finally constructed in 1972 and opened in August 1973. (Courtesy of HistoryMiami Museum.)

This photograph, taken in 1972, shows a greatly enhanced island through dredging and the erection of a bulkhead. Seven years earlier, the Claughtons received permission from the state to enlarge the island to 44 acres. Further, as the photograph indicates, construction of the all-important connecting bridge, which made possible the development of the island, is under way. (Courtesy of HistoryMiami Museum.)

This aerial photograph, taken in 1980 from south of the island, shows the first major building to be completed. At the same time, other parts of the island were being cleared for development as Swire Limited and Cheezem accelerated building activities. By the late 1990s, the development came to be known as Brickell Key on Claughton Island. (Casey M. Piket.)

As these photographs from the early 1980s show, the development of Claughton Island was under way. One of the keys behind its development was the completion, in August 1973, of the bridge connecting the island to the mainland with funding provided by the Claughton family and a new island ownership partner, Frates Properties of Tulsa, Oklahoma. The building seen in these photographs, the result of Swire Limited and Cheezem properties, which had purchased the Frates ownership interest, was a residential condominium called Brickell Key One and was completed in the fall of 1982. Development on the island was stalled after the completion of the first building but resumed in 1990, with the completion of numerous others, including the Courvosier Centre in 1990, Brickell Key II in 1991, and the Mandarin Oriental in 2000. The island today is nearly built out. (Both, courtesy of HistoryMiami Museum.)

Three

South Bayshore Drive

This aerial view is looking west toward the Brickell and Bulmer Apartments in the 1930s. During Prohibition, bootleggers would unload liquor imported from the Bahamas on the dock seen here. Miami was considered the "leakiest" city in America during Prohibition. (Courtesy of State Library and Archives of Florida.)

This is a view of the Brickell apartments looking west from Biscayne Bay. They were built by the Brickells' second oldest son, Charles, in 1916 at the eastern terminus of Southeast Eighth Street. The apartments opened in January 1917 and provided much needed housing for the rapidly growing city of Miami during World War I. (Photograph by Claude C. Matlack; courtesy of HistoryMiami Museum.)

Pictured are the Bulmer Apartments looking northwest from Southeast Eighth Street in the 1920s. This complex was built by William Brickell III, William and Mary Brickell's oldest son, across the street from the Brickell Apartments. The apartments were a tribute to Mary Brickell's maiden name. The first guest at the apartments was famed artist Louis Comfort Tiffany. (Photograph by Claude C. Matlack; courtesy of HistoryMiami Museum.)

Pictured are the Brickell Apartments looking southwest from the front driveway in 1956. The architect was George L. Pfeiffer, and the design was an adaptation of Neoclassical Mediterranean. There were 24 spacious apartments in the building. The floor plans consisted of one to four bedroom configurations, and each apartment had a private bath, hot water, electric lights, and its own balcony. The apartments provided an unobstructed view of downtown Miami from its rooftop until the Bulmer Apartments were built in 1919. The apartments were bought and sold several times from 1920 through the mid-1950s. Restaurateur Charles Creighton planned on building a waterfront restaurant here to provide a Miami location of his successful eatery in Fort Lauderdale, but was not able to raise enough money. (Courtesy of Miami-Dade Public Library, Romer Collection.)

The Bulmer Apartments are seen here in the 1970s. While the building was more than 50 years old, it stood until the end of the 1970s. The structure was originally designed to be nine stories, but a shortage of construction materials during and after World War I forced William Brickell to stop construction when the building reached three stories. The building featured rich ornamentation and two three-story towers with pyramidal roofs on each side, and the entrance consisted of a central pavilion with six Corinthian columns. Brickell and his wife, Olive, and son William IV moved into the apartments when they opened in 1919. Olive occupied the building long after it stopped operating as apartments and until her passing in March 1966. The property was sold to Flagship Bank in the early 1970s. (Courtesy of HistoryMiami Museum.)

Pictured is the demolition of the Brickell Apartments in January 1961. The beauty and tranquility of Charles Brickell's apartments began to fade after three decades of service to the Southside neighborhood. Charles Brickell died in 1924, and his ornate building was bought and sold several times over the next 30 years. The building was condemned by the city in the late 1950s. (Casey M. Piket.)

The demolition of the Bulmer Apartments is seen here in July 1978. After the acquisition of the building in the early 1970s, Flagship Bank did a feasibility study to see if it could adapt the apartment building as a central part of its commercial building. Preservation groups tried to protect the building from demolition, but the bank got its permit, and the apartments were razed. (Casey M. Piket.)

Pictured is the Four Ambassadors building on South Bayshore Drive in 1967. During the construction of the Four Ambassadors Hotel and Condominiums, the site was a filming location for the movie *Tony Rome*. In the scene pictured here, Frank Sinatra is meeting with his client at a job site. The Four Ambassadors was completed in 1967 and opened in January 1968. On February 19, 1968, the hotel was host to the Southern Christian Leadership Conference that featured Martin Luther King Jr. leading nonviolence workshops. The conference in Miami was little more than six weeks prior to the assassination of Dr. King in Memphis, Tennessee, on April 4, 1968. The Four Ambassadors was partially built on land formerly occupied by the Brickell Apartments. (Dr. Paul S. George.)

Pictured is the Four Ambassadors from an empty lot in 1968. When the hotel opened in January 1968, it served both as a hotel and apartment complex. The immediate area around the buildings was mostly undeveloped. The buildings were on South Bayshore Drive, which was extended from Southeast Eighth Street to Southeast Twelfth Street a few years earlier. (Dr. Paul S. George.)

This is an aerial view, looking northeast, of the Brickell neighborhood in 1968. The foreground features the Four Ambassadors and provides an excellent view of the amenities along the bayfront. There were two pools and several restaurants that catered to hotel guests and residents. Brickell Avenue is to the west of the complex. (Dr. Paul S. George.)

This is South Bayshore Drive in the 1950s. This unique aerial view highlights the Ocean Ranch Motel (foreground) along with garden apartments and residences in the Brickell neighborhood in mid-century Miami. The Ocean Ranch began in a former mansion built for the Pearson family in the mid-1920s. The motel portion was south of the original building, across the street on Southeast Twelfth Street, a two-story structure with cabanas around the pool area. South of the motel, on the same side of the street, were the Bayshore Drive Apartments. This building was originally called the Fredora Apartments when it opened in November 1922, based on the names of the couple who built and ran the apartments, Fred and Dora Brown. (Casey M. Piket.)

This is the front entrance of the Wyeth residence in 1925. Walter B. Pearson, president of the Chicago-based Standard Screw Company, commissioned Gordon Mayer to design this mansion in 1917. However, Pearson died before construction began. It was sold to businessman Huston Wyeth and later to Harry Dewitt, who converted it into the main building for the Ocean Ranch Motel complex in the mid-1940s. (Courtesy of the Miami-Dade Public Library, Romer Collection.)

This is Southeast Twelfth Street looking east toward the Ocean Ranch Motel sign at the edge of the bay on July 19, 1951. The motel was a sprawling complex that included a Neoclassic Mediterranean mansion (left) and a swimming pool with cabanas and motel rooms. The motel was advertised as a family-friendly destination and was host to fashion and water shows. (Courtesy of the Miami-Dade Public Library, Romer Collection.)

The Ocean Ranch Motel pool was a popular place for guests to enjoy beautiful winter afternoons and evenings. Neighborhood schoolchildren learned how to swim in this pool, and visitors and residents fondly remember the active social calendar that was hosted on the pool deck and around the cabanas during the 1950s and 1960s. (Casey M. Piket.)

This was the home of Dr. James Jackson in 1905 in downtown Miami at the northeast corner of Flagler Street and Northeast Second Avenue. The Jacksons built their home in 1899 and lived in it until 1916, when it was moved to Southeast Twelfth Terrace in today's Brickell neighborhood. (Courtesy of the State Library and Archives of Florida.)

Here is Dr. Jackson's surgical center and office in 1905, the same year it was built along Northeast Second Avenue behind his residence. There was a walkway connecting this building with the residence. The hitching post on the right was moved to the Miami City Cemetery near Dr. Jackson's gravesite when he was interred in 1924. Dr. Jackson had segregated waiting rooms at the front of the building. His examination office, surgery room, and office were in the rear. This building was moved in 1916 to Southeast Twelfth Street in the Brickell neighborhood. After it was moved, it was no longer used as a doctor's office. Today, it is the office of Dade Heritage Trust. (Courtesy of the State Library and Archives of Florida.)

The Jackson home is waiting to be moved by barge in 1916. Both the residence and surgical center were placed on rollers and guided down Flagler Street to the water's edge, where they were placed on barges. At the time the buildings were moved off their downtown lots, the Jacksons did not have a buyer for either structure. Dr. Jackson planned to move them to a lot he owned on Miami Beach when H.T. Whaler, a pioneer jeweler, decided to buy both the home and office and move them to two lots he owned on today's Southeast Twelfth Street. By the mid-1960s, both the office and residence had been converted to rooming houses and had fallen into a state of disrepair. The Jackson residence remained at its Southeast Twelfth Street address until it was razed in June 2001. (Courtesy of HistoryMiami Museum.)

Dr. Jackson's surgical center and home is pictured here on Southeast Twelfth Street in the Brickell neighborhood in 1979. Both buildings had been used as rooming houses for new immigrants fleeing Fidel Castro's Cuba. Despite having ties to an important Miami pioneer, the residence was in such poor condition that it was considered unsalvageable by the late 1990s. (Courtesy of HistoryMiami Museum.)

Dade Heritage Trust is seen here in 2018. The preservation society restored Dr. Jackson's surgical center and used it as an office beginning in 1977. The building is still standing on the same corner where it was moved in 1916 and continues to be maintained and occupied by Dade Heritage Trust as its headquarters. (Courtesy of Dade Heritage Trust.)

The demolition of Dr. Jackson's residence at 186 Southeast Twelfth Street is shown on June 6, 2001. After a fire broke out in June 2000, the building was condemned. A preservation battle between Dade Heritage Trust and the property owner ensued. By summer of 2001, the battle was lost, and the residence was demolished. (Courtesy of Dade Heritage Trust.)

These are the front steps to Dr. Jackson's former residence during demolition. By the end of the day, only these steps and a pile of rubble remained. The Solaris at Brickell condominiums now sit on the site. (Courtesy of Dade Heritage Trust.)

Shown are two office buildings under construction along Brickell Bay Drive in the mid-1980s. With the construction of office space during this time, the neighborhood developed a reputation as a financial district due to banks and insurance organizations leasing significant space in these buildings. The building in the foreground was One Brickell Square at 801 Brickell Avenue, which became the regional headquarters of Mastercard International when it opened in 1986. The office building under construction in the background, to the south of the Four Ambassadors, is 1001 South Bayshore Drive (now Brickell Bay Drive), which also opened in 1986. (Courtesy of HistoryMiami Museum.)

Brickell's developing skyline is in the background of this photograph of a busy Miami River. (Courtesy of HistoryMiami Museum.)

Four

Brickell Avenue from Miami River to Point View

Much of the allure of the Brickell Avenue of the past stems from its natural beauty and its uniquely built environment featuring grand homes with Neoclassical touches. The Miss Harris Florida School exemplified both of these virtues with its outdoor classes near the edge of sparkling Biscayne Bay and its beautiful columned main building. (Courtesy of State Library and Archives of Florida.)

These photographs of Brickell Avenue in its early days hearken to a time in the late 19th century when the area was bereft of people. The avenue itself was created at the behest of Mary Brickell, who, along with her family, owned the property it traversed. In the late 19th century, under her direction, laborers cut a trail south through the thick hammock to connect the family's property and trading post to an existing road, today's South Bayshore Drive, which ran along the shore of Biscayne Bay, and the rising community of Coconut Grove, five miles south of the mouth of the Miami River. (Both, courtesy of Larry Wiggins.)

Brickell Avenue had already taken on a polish by 1913, as handsome residences appeared along the thoroughfare that two decades earlier was a rough path through a subtropical hammock. Additional homes would continue to rise on Brickell Avenue as it took its place as one of the fledgling city's most beautiful, affluent neighborhoods by the mid-1920s. (Courtesy of HistoryMiami Museum.)

The mighty hurricane of 1926 spared few parts of Miami. The verdant Brickell Avenue neighborhood suffered both heavy building and tree damage from winds of more than 130 miles per hour. Few were prepared for the effects of the storm, or its economic aftermath. (Courtesy of Miami-Dade Public Library, Romer Collection.)

Taken by famed photographer Gleason Waite Romer in 1927, these photographs capture the natural beauty of the Brickell Avenue neighborhood, a carryover from its earlier era as a subtropical hammock. Though the hammock was gone in much of the northern part of the neighborhood, remnants of it were alive and well south of Southeast Fifteenth Road, especially in Jungle Park, later renamed Simpson Park, one of Miami's earliest parks. Farther south, other undeveloped areas were still hammock land. It was this hammock, or "woodlands," along with the waters of nearby Biscayne Bay, that set the neighborhood apart from other parts of Miami. (Both, courtesy of Miami-Dade Public Library, Romer Collection.)

Brickell Avenue is seen here looking south from Southeast Tenth Street in 1927. The thoroughfare possesses all of the qualities that Mary Brickell wanted for her namesake avenue, including a wide and beautifully landscaped median. At the time of this photograph, the avenue ended at the Miami River, as can be seen here with a clear view of Henry Flagler's Royal Palm Hotel in the distance on the north side of the river. (Courtesy of the Miami-Dade Public Library System, Romer Collection.)

The early-20th-century homes that arose on Brickell Avenue were of heroic size and bore attractive architectural designs, as seen in this photograph of the domicile of William Brickell III, which was built in 1910. William and his family lived in this home for nine years before they moved into the Bulmer Apartments when it opened in 1919. This residence and its property were purchased by the Claughton family in the mid-1950s, and by 1958, it was razed and replaced with an office building and garden apartments. The home was a wood-frame structure, which was very common in Miami's Southside neighborhood at the time. The neighborhood's early residences were still standing into the early post–World War II period, but by the 1960s, many of them had disappeared, replaced by small apartment complexes, motels, and mid-rise commercial buildings. (Courtesy of HistoryMiami Museum.)

This is Charles Brickell's residence at 823 Brickell Avenue in May 1955. Charles was Bill and Mary Brickell's second oldest son and owned the block of property along the family's namesake avenue from Southeast Eighth Street to Southeast Tenth Street, east to Biscayne Bay. Charles built this two-story, six-room home in 1911 on the corner of Southeast Eighth Street and Brickell Avenue. He died unexpectedly in the home in August 1924 after returning from travel in Pennsylvania. His widow, Fannie, and their son James lived here for years following Charles's death, but the house was condemned and razed following a fire in the late 1950s. (Courtesy of HistoryMiami Museum.)

Pictured is the US Department of Agriculture (USDA) Experimental Station in 1916. The station was placed in the Brickell neighborhood at the request of Dr. David Fairchild, a renowned botanist who lived in Coconut Grove, to introduce nonindigenous subtropical plants into the South Florida environs. The property spanned from Biscayne Bay to South Miami Avenue along the 1100 block of Brickell Avenue. (Courtesy of the State Library and Archives of Florida.)

By 1926, the station had outgrown its location on Brickell Avenue, which led to the USDA moving it to Coconut Grove. Many of the plants and trees cultivated there were transplanted to other parts of Miami, including the Miami City Cemetery. Dr. David Fairchild referred to the experimental station as the "Ellis Island for plants." (Courtesy of the State Library and Archives of Florida.)

Founded in the early 1900s in Coconut Grove, the Miss Harris Florida School, named for its founder Julia Harris, moved in 1916 to a converted residence at the southwest corner of Southeast Eighth Street and Brickell Avenue. The building at this location was constructed by the Brickell family and rented to the school while it constructed a permanent home farther south. This was also the temporary home of William Jennings Bryan while his Villa Serena mansion was being built in 1912. The structure seen here was built in 1922, and became a fixture in the community as many of Miami's most prominent families enrolled their daughters in the school. In 1957, feeling the city around the school had grown too big, Julia Harris moved to Palm City, Florida. (Courtesy of State Library and Archives of Florida.)

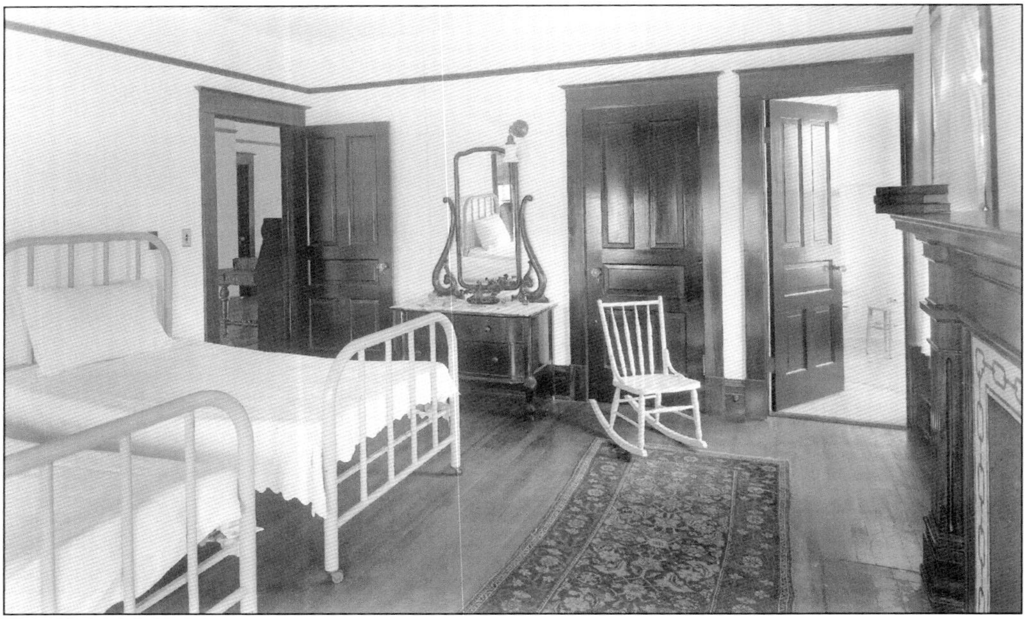

This photograph from 1922 shows a bedroom used as a dormitory for boarding students of the Miss Harris Florida School. The school contained a mix of both boarders and day students. Initially, it was open only to girls but later accepted male students, including William Brickell IV and the future longtime mayor of Miami Maurice Ferre. (Courtesy of State Library and Archives of Florida.)

Miss Harris's school maintained a dominant presence on Brickell Avenue from the late 1910s until it was moved to Palm City in 1957. The school occupied a beautiful wood frame home but also offered outdoor classes in screened gazebos that backed to the beautiful waters of Biscayne Bay. (Courtesy of the Miami-Dade Public Library, Romer Collection.)

This 1925 photograph shows the Rendezvous Tea Room at 1305 Brickell Avenue in the 1920s. This was the former residence of Carl Fisher, the father of Miami Beach, and his wife, Jane, who named the property The Shadows due to the serenity provided by the stately royal palm trees. (Courtesy of the Miami-Dade Public Library, Romer Collection.)

The former Fisher home at 1305 Brickell Avenue was converted into the Whitehall Apartments in the mid-1940s. Once the former driveway of the residence was converted into Southeast Thirteenth Street, there was a roundabout installed to route traffic around the building. Many Brickell residents began referring to it as the "house in the middle of the street" until it was razed in the early 1970s. (Courtesy of HistoryMiami Museum.)

The First Presbyterian Church, one of Miami's first houses of worship, moved to a new facility at 609 Brickell Avenue in 1949. The prior location was in downtown Miami, on the corner of Flagler Street and Southeast Third Avenue, on land donated by Henry Flagler in 1900. The first service, conducted in a tent on the west side of today's South Miami Avenue along the Miami River, was held in 1896. The northern section of the church replicates part of the original building and includes the original dais and stained-glass windows, the latter reportedly created by Louis Comfort Tiffany. While the church has received countless offers to buy the property, it remains a vibrant congregation in the heart of the neighborhood. (Courtesy of Casey Piket.)

Designed by Robert Law Weed, the 550 Building in the 500 block of Brickell Avenue was completed in 1952. It represented a revolution in the changing landscape of Brickell Avenue since it was one of the first commercial buildings to arise on the verdant street. One of Brickell Avenue's tallest buildings at the time, the 550 Building showcased the fledgling Mid-Century Miami design. (Courtesy of HistoryMiami Museum.)

This view from the newly opened 550 Building in 1952 highlights the rustic nature of the Brickell Avenue neighborhood as well as the beautiful waters of Biscayne Bay. Because of its scale and height, the 550 Building stood out in the neighborhood. (Courtesy of HistoryMiami Museum.)

McLamore's Restaurant was in the 550 Building on Brickell Avenue. James McLamore was convinced to move to Miami and open a restaurant by his father-in-law, Dr. E. Sterling Nichol, founder of the Miami Heart Institute. The restaurant was known for "dinner bell Charlie," a boy who rang a bell outside during rush hour. McLamore sold the restaurant in 1954 to partner with Dave Edgerton in a hamburger restaurant franchise that would become Burger King. (Both, Casey M. Piket.)

This photograph of the Castlereagh Apartments, taken in 1951, shows the continued evolution of the Brickell Avenue neighborhood. Located at 1005 Brickell Avenue and built in the style of a retrofitted Brickell mansion, these apartments, which traced their beginnings to the era preceding World War II, served a growing number of seasonal visitors as well as long-term renters. The property extended as far east as the bay since there was no Brickell Bay Drive until the mid-1960s. The aforementioned thoroughfare was originally called South Bayshore Drive, but it was renamed by the Miami City Commission to Brickell Bay Drive in 2004 to eliminate confusion with the South Bayshore Drive farther south along the ridge providing access to Coconut Grove. One of the tenants in the late 1960s was future television and film star Victoria Principal. (Courtesy of Miami-Dade Public Library, Romer Collection.)

One of the more unusual apartment houses on Brickell Avenue in the mid-1900s was the Hanna Apartments. Dr. Fuad H. Hanna, who initially practiced medicine in downtown Miami, purchased a mansion at 1299 Brickell Avenue in 1935, then expanded and converted the home into an apartment complex. After selling that building to Dr. Luis Rivera in 1949, he purchased a mansion at 848 Brickell Avenue and converted it into the Hanna Apartments, pictured above. His medical office was adjoined to the apartments, providing the doctor with a very short commute to work; the Hanna family lived in one of the apartments. Pictured below are the doctor and his wife enjoying a nice winter afternoon in the backyard of the complex in December 1952. (Both, courtesy of Miami-Dade Public Library, Romer Collection.)

The South Winds Hotel, on the southwest corner of Brickell Avenue and Southeast Seventh Street, is seen here on March 29, 1951. Motels became very common on Brickell Avenue following World War II. The South Winds provided tourists with convenient overnight accommodations as they traveled south on Brickell Avenue, which was part of US Highway 1. (Casey M. Piket.)

By the early post–World War II era, parts of Brickell Avenue were undergoing a transformation as motels began to appear to accommodate the growing legion of visitors to Miami Beach and downtown Miami. The Arrowhead Motel, seen in this postcard based on a 1950s photograph, featured a sleek Streamline Moderne/Art Deco–styled office with a standard motel configuration. (Courtesy of Casey Piket.)

The Brickell Motel was located at 1177 Brickell Avenue and served as another example of how the avenue changed from family residences to motels. This trend began in the early 1950s, and many of the motels remained standing and viable through the 1980s, and some into the 1990s. (Casey M. Piket.)

The Towne Motel offers a graphic example of the Mid-Century Miami or Miami Moderne style that characterized the numerous motels and hotels throughout Greater Miami in the early post–World War II era. Featured here is a picturesque sign highlighted by neon illumination, masonry elements pointing toward the heavens, and an "eyebrow" over and along the side of the window on the left. (Courtesy of Casey Piket.)

This 1950s photograph shows the quickening pace of life on the once quiescent Brickell Avenue. While a portion of the median is bereft of trees, the east side of the street remains verdant. The towering 550 Building looms at right, but a half century later, it was razed to make room for Jorge Perez's 500 Brickell Condominium. (Courtesy of Casey Piket.)

Built in 1938 at a cost of $250,000, the Garden Lane Apartments represented an early break with the dominant single-family homes that graced Brickell Avenue. Designed by Coral Gables architect Upton Ewing, the apartment complex looked out over a beautiful garden with a fountain as a centerpiece. This photograph of the address sign was taken on July 19, 1951. (Courtesy of Miami-Dade Public Library, Romer Collection.)

This mid-1960s photograph shows the northern flow of traffic over the original Brickell Avenue Bridge into downtown. The bridge opened in 1930, providing a direct connection for the first time between the residential Brickell Avenue neighborhood and Miami's bustling center. In 1995, the bridge was replaced by a higher drawbridge adorned with sculptures of historical Miami figures. (Courtesy of Casey Piket.)

The venerable Flagship Bank is pictured shortly after it opened in 1980. Constructed in 1979 at a time when the office occupancy rate in Dade County was approaching 93 percent, the bank building provided much needed commercial space as financial institutions and other organizations sought office space in downtown Miami. (Courtesy of HistoryMiami Museum.)

This is 1221 Brickell, at the corner of Brickell Avenue and Southeast Twelfth Terrace, when it was completed in 1986. Its hexagonal glass and stainless-steel construction provides for up to 22 corner windows on each floor. This beautiful 27-story office tower appeared in several episodes of the television show *Miami Vice* in the 1980s. (Courtesy of HistoryMiami Museum.)

This photograph of the 550 Building, taken in 1981, provides another look at this early commercial structure on Brickell Avenue. Behind it stand other commercial buildings representing the rapidly changing makeup of the street. The 550 Building hosted the restaurant owned and operated by James McLamore, who sold it to purchase a fast food franchise in 1954. (Courtesy of HistoryMiami Museum.)

Today's beautifully landscaped Brickell Avenue was still a work in progress in 1981, as seen in this photograph of the northernmost blocks of the thoroughfare. New plantings and even a small monument to Mary Brickell would appear in subsequent decades. Traffic congestion had already begun to be an issue by the early 1980s. (Courtesy of HistoryMiami Museum.)

By 1982, the Brickell Avenue landscape had changed considerably from the period immediately following World War II. Mid-rise and high-rise structures now dotted the avenue as the result of a transformative building boom commencing in the late 1970s. The southern part of the neighborhood featured condominium towers, whereas the northern section saw the rise of commercial buildings as the avenue evolved into an international banking center. (Courtesy of HistoryMiami Museum.)

These photographs, taken in 1982 and 1984, illustrate the dynamic development of Brickell Avenue. These buildings would welcome new additions to the street on a regular basis from then until today, positioning Brickell Avenue as a dynamic center of residences, offices, and banking. Brickell showcased the area's most stunning architecture during each boom from the late 1970s on. It was their avant-garde designs for such condominiums as the Atlantis, The Palace, and the Imperial that catapulted Arquitectonica, founded in the mid-1970s, into the ranks of the world's great architectural firms. The two most recent booms, in the early 2000s, filled much of the available space in the neighborhood with new high-rises while pushing development deep into West Brickell. (Both, courtesy of State Library and Archives of Florida.)

This aerial view, looking north from Southeast Thirteen Street, highlights the maturity of Brickell Avenue by 1987. The circular building on the east side of the avenue (right), referred to as the "Roundhouse," was the office of the Nichols, Gaither, Green, Frates, and Beckham law firm beginning in 1959. Local television station WCIX operated out of this building from 1967 until the early 1980s. (Courtesy of HistoryMiami Museum.)

By the time this photograph was taken in 1993, little was left of Brickell Avenue's once posh residential community. Instead, the street and the city had grown vertically, paving the way for the emergence of the exciting Brickell Avenue neighborhood of today. (Casey M. Piket.)

Five

POINT VIEW

This is an aerial photograph of Point View in the late 1920s. The land that comprised this block was a swamp that many potential developers considered worthless. There were sections that were as much as five feet under water. Locke T. Highleyman saw the potential of the area and determined an approach to dredge the bay bottom to fill the waterlogged block and make it one of Miami's signature developments. (Courtesy of HistoryMiami Museum.)

Pictured at left is Locke T. Highleyman, developer of the Point View subdivision. He hailed from St. Louis, Missouri, and began traveling to Miami in 1902 as a winter visitor. He was a successful real estate developer in his hometown and frequented Miami to not only evade the cold winters of the Midwest, but also to find opportunity in a growing new city. Locke moved his family to Miami permanently in 1911 and embarked on developing the Point View subdivision of Brickell. Later, he also created and developed Palm and Hibiscus Islands in Biscayne Bay in partnership with Clarence Busch. Pictured below is Locke's wife, Kathryn Highleyman. She was very active in Miami's social circles and supported many civic organizations, including the Florida Historical Society, until her passing on February 20, 1979. (Both, courtesy of HistoryMiami Museum.)

Locke T. Highleyman purchased 28 acres of mostly swampland from the Brickell family in 1911. Although the acreage was under water by as much as five feet in some areas, Highleyman had a plan to fill and develop the land into what would become the upscale Point View neighborhood. Here, workers are laying pipes to prepare for development. (Courtesy of HistoryMiami Museum.)

This image shows the standing water that Highleyman needed to drain and fill. The southwest corner of Point View was more than five feet under water in 1911 when he began to prepare the land for development. He relied on the expertise of his neighbor G.F. Cook, who had experience dredging the St. John's River prior to moving to Miami. (Courtesy of HistoryMiami Museum.)

Pictured is the dredger at work using fill from the bay bottom to extend the eastern edge of Highleyman's property in 1913. The Florida Improvement Fund provided approval for developers to create land out of the bay bottom. Part of the land that resulted from the dredge and fill process created part of South Bayshore Drive, which was renamed Brickell Bay Drive in 2004. (Courtesy of HistoryMiami Museum.)

This retaining wall was built during the construction of Point View. This photograph was also taken in 1913, but much later in the year. The familiar curve of Brickell Bay Drive was starting to develop at this point in the process. (Courtesy of HistoryMiami Museum.)

This photograph was taken in 1913 in the middle of today's Southeast Fourteenth Street. The road was originally called Kathryn Street in honor of the matriarch of the Highleyman family, but was changed as part of the Chaille street naming system approved in the fall of 1920 by the Miami City Council. In this photograph, Kathryn stands in the middle of her namesake road surrounded by palm trees. (Courtesy of the Daly Highleyman Collection.)

Locke Highleyman stands next to his car on Kathryn Street in 1913. The Highleymans were part of a caravan of automobiles that traveled from Jacksonville to Miami in 1911, ending in front of the Royal Palm Hotel, prior to there being paved roads along that route. The couple had to navigate a variety of terrain to complete the journey. (Courtesy of HistoryMiami Museum.)

The west side of the 1400 block of Brickell Avenue is seen here in 1914. While not located within the boundaries of the subdivision, this portion of Brickell Avenue between Fourteenth Street and Fifteenth Road was unofficially considered part of Point View. The home under construction at the time of this photograph had an address of 1446 Brickell Avenue and was built by the Brickells for Capt. James Franklin Jaudon, who was instrumental in the completion of the Tamiami Trail to Miami. The small home to its north, with an address of 1438 Brickell Avenue, was built for Jaudon's brother Paul Jaudon. The home at 1446 Brickell was later bought and occupied by Miami pioneer judge Andrew J. Rose until his widow sold it to theater and real estate investor Edward Claughton in 1944. The large home at far left had an address of 1452 Brickell Avenue, and was on the corner of Brickell Avenue and Fifteenth Road. It was purchased by R. Freeman Burdine in 1921 and remained in his family until 1966. (Courtesy of HistoryMiami Museum.)

The first home that Locke T. Highleyman built for his family in Point View is seen here. It was designed by August Geiger in Neoclassical Mediterranean style and was located at 1412 South Bay Shore Drive. Highleyman sold it to New York retailer James P. Logan in 1916. The home was named Chateau Reve, French for "dream castle." (Courtesy of HistoryMiami Museum.)

Here is a spec home built by Highleyman in 1915 at 1402 South Bay Shore drive in Point View. Although the Highleymans never lived in this home, they financed its construction to provide a model for the types of residences that could be found in the subdivision. It was sold to the president of the company that sold Father John's Medicine in Lowell, Massachusetts. (Casey M. Piket.)

Pictured are the mansions at 1412 and 1408 South Bay Shore Drive in Point View. The residence in the foreground was Highleyman's first family home, Chateau Reve. Following the death of the next owner, James P. Logan, in 1922, the property changed hands several times until Wade Harley purchased it in 1927. Harley was a real estate developer who worked with Carl Fisher to help develop Miami Beach. The residence in the background was built in 1915 by Edwin McGraw, president of the McGraw Tire and Rubber Company. The home was later owned by Eugene Staley of Decatur, Illinois, from 1930 until his passing in 1940. Staley was best known as the owner of a professional football team called the Decatur Staleys, which would later be moved to Chicago and renamed the Bears. (Casey M. Piket.)

This postcard shows 1418 South Bay Shore Drive in Point View. It was the second Highleyman residence designed by August Geiger. Locke Highleyman moved his family into this home and lived there briefly before he sold it to Charles F. McGilvary of Springfield, Ohio, in 1918. (Courtesy of Larry Wiggins.)

Sailors from Dinner Key Naval Air Station enjoy a meal with the Highleymans at their mansion at 1418 South Bay Shore Drive. The air base, located in Coconut Grove, was established to prepare naval aviators for battle during World War I. (Courtesy of HistoryMiami Museum.)

This postcard shows an aerial view of Point View looking east to west from South Bay Shore Drive. From left to right are two homes designed by August Geiger for the Highleyman family, and the Edwin McGraw mansion, which featured a six-car garage with two apartments above it. (Courtesy of Casey Piket.)

This is the residence built by C.L. Craig in 1914 at 94 Southeast Fourteenth Street in Point View. This style of home was typical of the dwellings constructed in the subdivision during the second and third decades of the 20th century. This grand domicile was constructed as a spec home to highlight the opulence of the neighborhood. As the reputation of Point View grew, Highleyman sold lots to general contractors, who built homes similar to this in anticipation of selling to a wealthy buyer at a later date. Craig sold this Point View home to Maude and Edward Z. Duncan, a retired executive from the Northern Pipeline Company of Oil City, Pennsylvania, in 1915. (Courtesy of HistoryMiami Museum.)

Pictured is the third and last residence built by Locke Highleyman in Point View, at 1420 South Bay Shore Drive. The family lived in this mansion for less than a year in 1919, when Highleyman opted to rent it to William H. Luden of Reading, Pennsylvania, the creator of the menthol cough drop. Highleyman sold this property to Luden in February 1920. (Courtesy of HistoryMiami Museum.)

Pictured is a dance in the backyard of the Luden mansion in the early 1920s. Despite the strictures of Prohibition, the residents of Point View entertained and enjoyed the spoils of the Roaring Twenties. Homeowners in this affluent subdivision were more apt to entertain at their homes to showcase their beautiful residences. (Courtesy of HistoryMiami Museum.)

The view of South Bayshore Drive above is looking north from the curve of Point View's distinctive street on September 17, 1919. At the time of this photograph, the subdivision was seven years old and developing rapidly. At left is Chateau Reve at 1412 Bay Shore Drive and the McGraw mansion at 1408 Bay Shore Drive. The picture below is a similar view from 1925. In both, the landscaping is distinctively South Florida, and the foliage along South Bayshore Drive had matured quickly since the subdivision's beginning. (Both, courtesy of HistoryMiami Museum and Miami-Dade Public Library System, Romer Collection.)

This is the second home built by Locke T. Highleyman, located at 1418 South Bay Shore Drive. This 12-room structure included a multicar garage and servant's quarters. Locke built his second family residence when James P. Logan, founder of one of New York's largest white goods establishments, made an offer in February 1916 to purchase his first home for $50,000, which provided a handsome profit. The Highleymans moved into their second residence in November 1916 and lived there until they accepted an unsolicited offer to sell the home to Fred C. McGilvray, a former mayor of Springfield, Ohio, in 1918. (Courtesy of Larry Wiggins.)

Pictured above is a home built by William Clifford at 1415 Brickell Avenue. This beautiful residence was named Netherby after the Cliffords' villa in Croydon, England. The villa was destroyed in a bomb raid by a German zeppelin in November 1915 during World War I. Clifford made his fortune in steel and was based in Pittsburgh, Pennsylvania, when not vacationing at his Point View home during the winter. The Cliffords sold this mansion to Benjamin Adriance of New York City for $35,000 in April 1918. Adriance built his wealth as the president and owner of the Savage Arms company and as founder of the Adriance Machine Company. Below is the Adriance residence on September 17, 1920. (Both, courtesy of HistoryMiami Museum.)

Both of these photographs indicate how quickly the Point View subdivision and surrounding Brickell neighborhood matured over the course of the 1920s. Above is an aerial view looking southwest in the early 1920s, when the foliage and landscaping were taking root. Below is an aerial view looking northwest in the late 1920s, when the area had clearly matured. Some of the structures visible were not built at the time the first picture was taken. Along with the areas south of Fifteenth Road, Point View was considered part of the Gold Coast of Miami by the end of the decade. (Both, courtesy of Larry Wiggins.)

These photographs illustrate the beauty of the grounds and streets of the maturing subdivision. Above is South Bay Shore Drive looking south from Southeast Fourteenth Street in 1925. Most of the homes along this scenic street were built 10 years earlier and provided the beautiful vistas that Locke T. Highleyman envisioned when he purchased the land from the Brickells. Below is Southeast Fourteenth Street looking west from Brickell Avenue in 1926, prior to the great hurricane in September of that year. Both photographs convey the tranquility of the area that was so attractive to wealthy Northerners who invested in Miami during this era. (Both, courtesy of Miami-Dade Public Library, Romer Collection.)

This is an aerial view of Point View looking west in 1929. The beauty and opulence of the homes along South Bay Shore Drive are prominently displayed. South Bay Shore Drive was renamed by the Miami City Commission to Brickell Bay Drive in 2004. Southeast Fourteenth Street is at center and represents the southern boundary of Point View. Not visible is Fifteenth Road, which represents the northern boundary. This photograph was taken only three years after the devastating 1926 hurricane, which caused extensive damage to the trees and foliage in Point View. This image illustrates how quickly the landscaping recovered following the storm. (Courtesy of HistoryMiami Museum.)

This anchor chain fence surrounded the property at 1329 Brickell Avenue, a beautiful residence that was the longtime home of Emily Clark, a prominent citizen of Grand Rapids, Michigan. While she maintained her primary residence in Michigan, this home became her winter residence until her passing in 1929. The anchor chain was believed to have come from the USS *Maine*, a ship that was allegedly sunk in Havana Harbor and became one of the causes of the Spanish-American War in 1898. The story was later debunked when it was revealed that it was from a shipwrecked four-masted American schooner discovered off the coast of Tavernier in 1910. The salvaged anchor chain was sold to William Huffstetler and then later resold to Dale Miller, who built the home for Emily Clark. The chain attracted visitors who were curious about this unique fence. (Courtesy of Miami-Dade Public Library, Romer Collection.)

This was the view looking west from the intersection of Brickell Avenue and Southeast Fourteenth Street the day after the great hurricane of 1926. The eye of the storm passed near the Brickell neighborhood and caused a lot of damage. The home on the corner at left was 1329 Brickell Avenue, featuring the anchor chain fence. (Courtesy of Miami-Dade Public Library, Romer Collection.)

This photograph was taken on September 18 following the great hurricane of 1926. The view is looking north on South Bay Shore Drive in Point View. The powerful winds knocked down trees and light poles and thinned much of the beautiful tree canopy within the subdivision. (Courtesy of Miami-Dade Public Library, Romer Collection.)

This photograph was taken at the intersection Brickell Avenue and Fifteenth Road facing northwest in November 1934. While technically outside the boundaries of Point View, the homes on the west side of Brickell Avenue were considered part of the subdivision. (Courtesy of Miami-Dade Public Library, Romer Collection.)

This aerial photograph of Point View in 1950 highlights the maturity of the 35-year-old subdivision. Within 10 years, some of the fine residences along South Bay Shore Drive would be replaced with mid-rise multifamily cooperatives, which began to transform the subdivision. (Courtesy of HistoryMiami Museum.)

This was the home of Dr. John Turner at 1449 Brickell Avenue in the 1950s. The doctor purchased this residence in the mid-1930s, and the family owned the home until it was sold in the late 1960s to the architectural firm of Reiff-Feldman & Associates, which converted it into commercial office space. The Turners were active in the institutional life of their community, especially with the West Minister Presbyterian Church. (Courtesy of Laura Hemphill.)

The Turner family home is pictured again in this 1950s view looking southeast from Brickell Avenue and Southeast Fourteenth Street. The house to the south of the Turner home was originally built for G.F. Cook, who partnered with Highleyman to dredge and fill the land that became Point View. It was located at 1451 Brickell Avenue. (Courtesy of Laura Hemphill.)

Pictured here are the abandoned Commodore Row and Yacht Club and the rising Babylon Apartments on December 1, 1979. Construction of the apartment building was put on hold when the federal government seized the property as part of money laundering charges brought against Sunshine State Bank, which provided financing for the project. Formerly the longtime residence of the Fay family and an asset of the same financial institution, the row and yacht club were also seized. The building behind them is the Brickell Bay Tower Condominiums, which opened as a cooperative in 1964 and was later converted to condominiums. The Babylon Apartments were sold at auction and were completed in time to open in 1982. The former Commodore Row and Yacht Club building was razed in 1988 to make room for the Commodore Bay Condominiums, which were constructed in the mid-1990s. (Courtesy of HistoryMiami Museum.)

This photograph highlights the changes in Point View in the 1970s. It was taken on December 10, 1979, and shows one of the last residences remaining in the subdivision. Beginning in the mid-1960s, the beautiful homes of the 1910s and 1920s were replaced with mid-rise residential towers. (Courtesy of HistoryMiami Museum.)

Point View is seen here in 1981. Most of South Bay Shore Drive was transformed into condominium row as the mansions that once lined this beautiful bayside street were replaced with residential towers. (Courtesy of HistoryMiami Museum.)

Six

Brickell's Millionaire Row

Here is an aerial view of Millionaire Row looking west from Biscayne Bay in the mid-1940s. The mansions seen in this photograph were built in the early 1920s and were designed in the Mediterranean style. This section of the Brickell Avenue neighborhood was later known as "Little San Juan" due to the number of affluent Puerto Rican families who moved into these estates around this time. (Courtesy of HistoryMiami Museum.)

This is a postcard view of Brickell Avenue, south of Fifteenth Road, looking southwest from Biscayne Bay. The image highlights the ridge along the avenue that peaks at more than 20 feet above sea level. The peak of the ridge was once the location of the home of Polly Lewis, who was granted 40 acres by the king of Spain in 1805. (Casey M. Piket.)

Devils Punch Bowl, south of today's Twenty-Sixth Road, is on the property of 3007 Brickell Avenue, near the shoreline of Biscayne Bay. It provided fresh water from an underground spring for early settlers. (Courtesy of State Library and Archives of Florida.)

This is the Assumption Academy chapel, on the corner of Fifteenth Road and Brickell Avenue, during its construction in 1946. The academy was a convent that began operating in Brickell in 1942 out of the former residence of the late Arthur Brisbane, one of the best-known American newspaper editors of the 20th century. (Courtesy of HistoryMiami Museum.)

Pictured is the chapel of the Assumption Academy at 126 Southeast Fifteenth Road during its first Mass on November 22, 1946. The church was designed in Romanesque Gothic style by the architectural firm of Henry Dagit & Sons of Philadelphia, Pennsylvania. Today, it is St. Jude Melkite Greek Catholic Church, and it is the only building remaining from the campus of the academy. (Courtesy of HistoryMiami Museum.)

The backyard of the Briggs estate at 1581 Brickell Avenue is pictured here in 1919. The mansion was designed by Pittsburgh architect Gordon Mayer on behalf of Charles L. Briggs, who ran a very successful leather manufacturing company in Haverhill, Massachusetts. The home was featured in *American Architect and Architecture* magazine when it was constructed in 1919. (Casey M. Piket.)

This is another view from the backyard of the Briggs mansion looking northwest in 1919. The residence featured many technological advances for the time, including a refrigeration plant, incinerator, linen chute, and telephone system, none of which were commonly found in homes of that era. (Casey M. Piket.)

This view is from the north side of the Briggs mansion looking southwest in 1919. The property was densely landscaped with both natural and planted foliage, as seen here. The residence had an H-shape and was designed to optimize natural lighting in every room. (Casey M. Piket.)

Pictured are the servants' quarters and garage on the Briggs property in 1919. The building included laundry facilities, a water softener system, and a pressure storage tank to support the maintenance of the property. The Briggs family owned the residence for 11 years. New York financier Foster C. Coombs purchased it in April 1930 for $175,000. (Casey M. Piket.)

These pictures demonstrate the extravagance of the Briggs mansion. Both were taken as part of a photo shoot for *American Architect and Architecture* in 1919. Above is the loggia on the first floor, and below is the living room. The dining room, which was adjacent to the living room, featured 22-foot ceilings, and the common areas were decorated with Florentine ornamentation. The home was later used as the offices for developer Nicholas Morley until it was razed in 1979 to make room for his Villa Regina condominiums. (Both, Casey M. Piket.)

This 1942 view shows the Briggs mansion from Biscayne Bay. It was owned by the Cabassa family during this era, until they sold to Nicholas Morley in 1969. Jacob Cabassa was from Ponce, Puerto Rico, and was part of a prominent family in the sugar industry. He moved his family to Miami to purchase land to expand their sugar cane operation and to invest in other ventures. In addition to Cabassa, Pedro Seralles, representing a prominent rum and sugar family from Puerto Rico, also purchased a home on Millionaire Row along Brickell Avenue. Several other prominent Puerto Rican families moved to Brickell around the same time. (Casey M. Piket.)

Chateau Petit Douy at 1500 Brickell Avenue is seen here in 1985. Constructed on a bluff on the southwest corner of Brickell Avenue and Fifteenth Road in 1931, the mansion was built for two attorneys, John and Ethel (Sheila) Murrell, and designed by architect Martin Luther Hampton. Ethel had a strong influence on both the design and name of residence, given her desire to incorporate features of Ernest Roume's castle in the village of Douy. She visited the Roume family on several occasions and had very fond memories of the chateau. Ethel Murrell was very active in fighting for women's rights. The mansion was awarded local historic designation in April 1982. (Both, courtesy of HistoryMiami Museum.)

This is an aerial view of Palm Court at 1597 Brickell Avenue (left) and the Briggs mansion at 1581 Brickell Avenue (right) from Biscayne Bay looking west in the 1920s. Palm Court was built for William W. Wheeler of St. Joseph, Missouri, president of the Wheeler-Motter Mercantile Company. Wheeler was a longtime visitor to Miami during the winter months when he purchased property on Brickell Avenue and built his estate in 1919. Following his death in 1925, the home was purchased by Burr S. Potter, an executive with the Model Land Company, a firm that handled the real estate interests of the FEC Corporation. Other notable owners include Arthur Rogers, president of Rogers Lumber Company in Wisconsin, and Lewis M. Adams, founder of multiple book manufacturing companies in New York and Tennessee. (Courtesy of State Library and Archives of Florida.)

Pictured is the Nolan mansion at 1548 Brickell Avenue, located on the west side of the thoroughfare, in the 1930s. It was constructed in 1926 for George Nolan, president of Miami National Bank, and his family. The architect was J.C. Gault, who designed a three-story southern Colonial residence that included 20 rooms, six baths, and a portico supported by four Corinthian columns. (Courtesy of Dade Heritage Trust.)

This is the large living room on the first floor of the Nolan mansion. The interior was beautifully decorated, as seen in this 1930 photograph. Oil portraits of George and Mae Nolan can be seen on the back wall. (Courtesy of Miami-Dade Public Library, Romer Collection.)

By the late 1970s, George and Mae Nolan's adult children, Henriette Harris and George Nolan Jr., were the caretakers of the mansion at 1548 Brickell Avenue. This photograph, taken in 1979, shows the home after the portico and columns were removed at the insistence of city inspectors. (Courtesy of Dade Heritage Trust.)

Taken in January 2018, this photograph shows the Nolan mansion still standing and operating as shared office space called Hive Brickell. It later changed its name to the Nolan House to commemorate the family that built the residence in 1926. (Casey M. Piket.)

Dr. James Jackson's mansion at 1627 Brickell Avenue is seen here. After the Jackson family sold their property in downtown Miami, they purchased two lots on Brickell Avenue to build this estate. Dr. Jackson's wife, Ethel, was so captivated by the natural beauty of the foliage on the property that she named this residence Homewood. It sat at the top of the ridge and featured Corinthian columns on both the front and back as well as large bay windows to allow for natural light and unobstructed views of the bay. Following Dr. Jackson's death in 1924, the home was briefly rented by Bernard Gimbel, head of Gimbel Brothers Department Store, which owned Saks Fifth Avenue and was the creator of the Gimbel's Thanksgiving Day Parade in Philadelphia in 1920. (Courtesy of State Library and Archives of Florida.)

Above are Dr. James Jackson and friend Lewell S. Barker relaxing on the back patio of Homewood. The patio provided the family a view of the expansive and beautifully landscaped backyard, as well as a picturesque view of Biscayne Bay. Below is the interior of the Jacksons' downtown residence before they sold it in 1916. Many of the decorative elements and furniture were moved into the family's Brickell home. In 1977, Homewood was a filming location for *The Greatest*, which starred Muhammad Ali playing himself in the story of his early life. (Above, courtesy of State Library and Archives of Florida; below, courtesy of HistoryMiami Museum.)

Jose Ferre is pictured at Homewood on February 24, 1956. Ferre purchased the estate in 1952, and it remained in his family until it was sold for demolition in the late 1970s. The Ferres were part of another prominent Puerto Rican family who lived on Brickell's Millionaire Row when it was referred to as Little San Juan. The family patriarch was a businessman involved in many different ventures, including real estate development. He constructed the 30-story New World Tower on Biscayne Boulevard in 1965, which was the tallest building in Miami until 1972. He was also the father of Maurice Ferre, Miami's first Hispanic mayor, who served six terms from 1973 to 1985. (Both, courtesy of HistoryMiami Museum.)

Directly south of Homewood is a mansion at 1643 Brickell Avenue constructed for Charles Davol in 1931. Davol was the son of the founder of the Davol Rubber Company of Rhode Island, which was established in 1870 to manufacture medical equipment. The home was built where Polly Lewis's house one stood. She was granted land by the king of Spain in 1805. Lewis's land grant was assessed at 643 acres at the time Florida became a US territory in 1821. She sold her property to Richard Fitzpatrick in 1832, and no structure was built on the site until Davol constructed his home in 1931. This is a view of the rear of the house, looking east to west, in 2016. The residence is today part of the Santa Maria condominium complex. (Casey M. Piket.)

The mansion at 1643 Brickell Avenue is seen here in 2016. It was purchased by well-known Venezuelan architect Luis Malaussena in 1952 and upgraded and given the name Santa Maria by its new owner. Malaussena was from a family of architects and employed a style that was considered neo-traditional for mid-century Venezuela. He excelled at adapting his styles to municipal buildings such as schools, airports, and other public spaces. His daughter Mercedes married her neighbor Maurice Ferre in 1959. The couple made Santa Maria their family home following Luis Malaussena's passing in 1963. Ugo Colombo, a Miami real estate developer, purchased the home and property in 1993 to complete his collection of lots to build a residential tower. The 51-story Santa Maria condominium high-rise was completed and opened in 1997. The mansion was preserved and serves as a private clubhouse for the residents. (Casey M. Piket.)

Brickell's Millionaire Row is seen from Biscayne Bay in August 1946. From left to right are the Briggs mansion at 1581 Brickell Avenue, Palm Court at 1597 Brickell, Helen Freeland's estate at 1617 Brickell, Homewood at 1627 Brickell, and Santa Maria at 1643 Brickell. Helen Freeland was Dr. James and Ethel Jackson's youngest daughter, who built her house next door to Homewood in 1938. At the time of this photograph, Antonio Miranda of San Juan, Puerto Rico, was the resident of the Freeland estate. Puerto Rican businessman Jacob Cabassa was listed at 1581 Brickell Avenue in 1946, when Brickell's Millionaire Row became popular with affluent Puerto Ricans relocating to Miami. A few years later, Jose Ferre purchased Homewood, and Pedro Seralles purchased 1839 Brickell Avenue. (Courtesy of HistoryMiami.)

Pictured is the estate of Caroline J. Brownell at 1564 Brickell Avenue on May 8, 1949. The residence was designed by architect Gordon Mayer and was constructed in 1919. Like the Briggs mansion, which was also designed by Mayer, the home was featured in *American Architect* in 1920 as a showcase of Mayer's work. (Courtesy of HistoryMiami Museum.)

Shown here is the pergola on the property at 1564 Brickell Avenue. This structure was a common feature of a Gordon Mayer–designed mansion. In 1960, the property was purchased by H. Brice McDonald, a senior pilot for National Airlines who at Christmas would travel to New York and purchase toys to bring back for poor children in Miami. (Courtesy of HistoryMiami Museum.)

Above is the estate at 1809 Brickell Avenue. Designed by Walter DeGarmo, it was built for Dr. Harry A. Lawton, of Warren, Ohio, who was a frequent winter visitor to Miami beginning in the early 1890s. He was a regular guest at Henry Flagler's Royal Palm Hotel after it opened in January 1897. In 1904, he purchased 100 feet of bayfront property from Mary Brickell, where he built his estate on a 12-foot oolitic limestone bluff, prompting him to name his home Lawton Cliffs. The Lawton family owned the property from the time it was built until Mary P. Lawton's passing in 1930. It was later owned by Dr. Edwin C. Thomas, the longtime Dade County coroner. (Both, Casey M. Piket.)

This is the estate that was once located at 1839 Brickell Avenue in 1915. Designed by famed architect Walter DeGarmo, the home was constructed in 1913 for John H. Havlin, who owned Hotel Havlin, the Grand Opera House, and several other valuable properties in Cincinnati, Ohio. Havlin built his estate in Miami after spending the winter of 1912 in the city. He was in poor health and wanted to find the ideal climate for his recovery. He named his estate Bon Air and built it on the same elevation as Lawton Cliffs, which was on the lot to the north. The property had 50 feet of frontage on the bay and a depth of 700 feet. The home was later owned by Chicago businessman David G. Joyce and then Puerto Rican Pedro J. Seralles. (Casey M. Piket.)

Pictured is Louis Tiffany's Comfort Lodge at 1865 Brickell Avenue in 1922. Tiffany was an internationally famous artist who specialized in working with stained glass. Traveling to South Florida on his private railcar, he was a frequent visitor to Miami. He decided to build his winter estate on Brickell's Millionaire Row in 1920 when his sister Annie Mitchell purchased property along the avenue and convinced him to do the same. The home was designed by Tiffany and was referred to as one of the oddest-looking structures by one of his neighbors while it was being constructed. Resembling a three-story tree fort, it was in the shape of an octagon and featured an observation deck on the third level where Tiffany could view Biscayne Bay above the tree line. (Both, courtesy of State Library and Archives of Florida.)

This postcard shows the home of Francis S. Whitten at 1887 Brickell Avenue from Biscayne Bay. Whitten was president of Columbia Phonograph in Wilmington, Delaware, and invested more than $250 million in real estate in South Florida beginning in 1919, the same year he constructed this mansion along Millionaire Row in Brickell. (Casey M. Piket.)

Pictured is the front of the estate at 1887 Brickell Avenue in 1925. The thicket of foliage in the front yard provided both beauty and privacy as the driveway led from Brickell Avenue to the residence on top of the bluff along the eastern section of the lot overlooking Biscayne Bay. (Courtesy of Miami-Dade Public Library, Romer Collection.)

Above is the backyard of 1887 Brickell Avenue, and below is the pool at the top of the bluff adjacent to the main house. The height of the ridge offered protection from high tides but did not keep homeowners from accessing and enjoying Biscayne Bay. Many of the homes along Millionaire Row had docks, providing residents easy access to their watercraft of choice. Both pictures were taken in 1925, the year that Francis Whitten sold this property to James Gilman, president of the Biscayne Trust Company, which owned the Bank of Bay Biscayne. The Gilmans owned the property from 1925 through the 1940s. (Both, courtesy of Miami-Dade Public Library, Romer Collection.)

The front entrance to Bay Terrace at 1927 Brickell Avenue is pictured in 1926. The estate was constructed for Miami pioneer Ralph Worthington, who began visiting the Magic City in 1897, one year after its incorporation. Worthington grew up on Euclid Avenue in Cleveland, Ohio, the same street where J.D. Rockefeller, Henry Flagler, Julia Tuttle, and the Brickells once lived. He was one of the first residents of Fort Dallas Park in downtown Miami after Harry Tuttle created the subdivision. He purchased the property to build Bay Terrace in 1919 and moved into the residence in 1920. The Worthingtons lived in the home until the mid-1940s, when they sold it to Edna Rickmers. Prior to purchasing Bay Terrace, Edna Rickmers lived at 609 Brickell Avenue until she sold that property to the First Presbyterian Church. (Both, courtesy of Miami-Dade Public Library, Romer Collection.)

These pictures capture the raw beauty of the Mitchell Bingham residence at 2025 Brickell Avenue along Millionaire Row. The home was built for Annie Mitchell, sister of Louis Comfort Tiffany and daughter of Charles L. Tiffany, founder of the noted New York city jewelry store. Owing to the many guava trees on the property from which the previous owner made a great deal of jelly, the home was given the name Sweet Way after the Mitchells purchased the property. When the home was being constructed, Annie Mitchell used the same general contractor as her brother, who was building the Comfort Lodge a few lots north. She instructed the contractor not to listen to Louis when he offered suggestions to improve her home because she did not want her residence to look anything like her brother's. (Both, courtesy of HistoryMiami Museum.)

Pictured is Sweet Way at 2025 Brickell Avenue in 1982. At the time of this photograph, the property had been mostly cleared for redevelopment, leaving only part of the residence and the bridge between the two wings. The home and land were sold to a Canadian firm that built the 21-story Atlantis Condominium on the property. The high-rise was one of several towers designed by the architectural firm Arquitectonica that replaced mansions along Millionaire Row beginning in the early 1980s. The Atlantis project broke ground on August 14, 1980, and construction was completed by 1982. The building is probably best known for being featured in the opening credits of *Miami Vice*. The complex incorporated part of the former Mitchell Bingham residence into the ground-level pool design by leaving and restoring the bridge seen here. (Courtesy of HistoryMiami Museum.)

The exterior of the residence known as Cocolobis at 2127 Brickell Avenue is shown here in 1935. This mansion was built for Maude Brickell in 1921; however, less than a year after its construction, it was leased to Pittsburgh businessman Charles J. Holleman after he purchased land west of Brickell Avenue to develop. Holleman had ambitious plans for what is still referred to as the Holleman Park subdivision, in today's Roads neighborhood. However, he died in a car accident on Brickell Avenue on August 20, 1923. The development was completed by his business partners, and the historic South Miami Avenue is central to the Holleman Park subdivision. Below is the interior of Cocolobis in 1935. (Both, courtesy of Saint Rosemund.)

Here are two additional photographs of the mansion at 2127 Brickell Avenue in 1935 showcasing the natural beauty around the residence. The home was named Cocolobis because there were so many pigeon plum trees on the property, and the botanical name for pigeon plum is *cocolobo*. The home was acquired by George C. Estill, president of Florida Power and Light, and his family in 1935. Below, the Estill women are enjoying a beautiful Miami winter day in 1935. Cocolobis was one of the last mansions still standing along Brickell's Millionaire Row when it was purchased and razed in the late 1980s. (Both, courtesy of Saint Rosemund.)

This postcard shows the home built for Amelia Elizabeth White at 3007 Brickell Avenue in 1936. White lived an extraordinary life that began in New York but led her to Santa Fe, New Mexico. She and her sister Martha settled in Santa Fe in 1923 and became great benefactors of the arts and archaeology of the Southwest. There is still a park named after her in Santa Fe. When White built her Brickell estate, she named it Fons Praedonum, Latin for "Robber's Spring," to pay homage to the legend of the Devil's Punch Bowl. It was believed that the spring was a gathering place for pirates and others seeking fresh water. The property sits on a 20-foot ridge with 483 feet of shoreline along Biscayne Bay. This opulent residence was bought by Hunter M. Bennett, an attorney and coal mine operator from Weston, West Virginia, in April 1944 for $54,000. Today, it is worth over $9 million. (Casey M. Piket.)

The postcard above shows the residence at 3031 Brickell Avenue, two blocks north of Vizcaya on Millionaire Row. The mansion was built in 1916 for Clarence Busch, business partner of Locke T. Highleyman during the creation and development of Palm and Hibiscus Islands. Busch was the real estate agent who unknowingly sold 93 Palm Avenue to Al Capone in 1928. (Casey M. Piket.)

Pictured here in the 1920s, this swimming pool in the backyard of 3031 Brickell Avenue was made of marble. Busch sold the residence and its furnishings to James Stanley Joyce, Chicago lumberman and brother of David Joyce, for $250,000 in January 1920. Joyce presented the home to his wife, actress Peggy Hopkins, as a wedding gift. (Casey M. Piket.)

The mansion at 3115 Brickell Avenue was the winter estate of William Jennings Bryan and was called Villa Serena. Bryan was a three-time candidate for president of the United States (1896, 1900, and 1908) and secretary of state (1913–1015) in the first term of Woodrow Wilson's presidency. He was a frequent visitor to Miami and often conducted Sunday sermons in Royal Palm Park and lectures at the Venetian Pool in 1924, helping George Merrick promote Coral Gables. The home, designed by August Geiger, was constructed in 1913 and became a place the Bryans loved to entertain other prominent Miami residents. The Bryans moved from Villa Serena to Coconut Grove in 1924. In 1932, the home was sold for $30,000 to William F. Cheek, the founder of the Maxwell House coffee company (Above, courtesy of State Library and Archives of Florida; below, Casey M. Piket.)

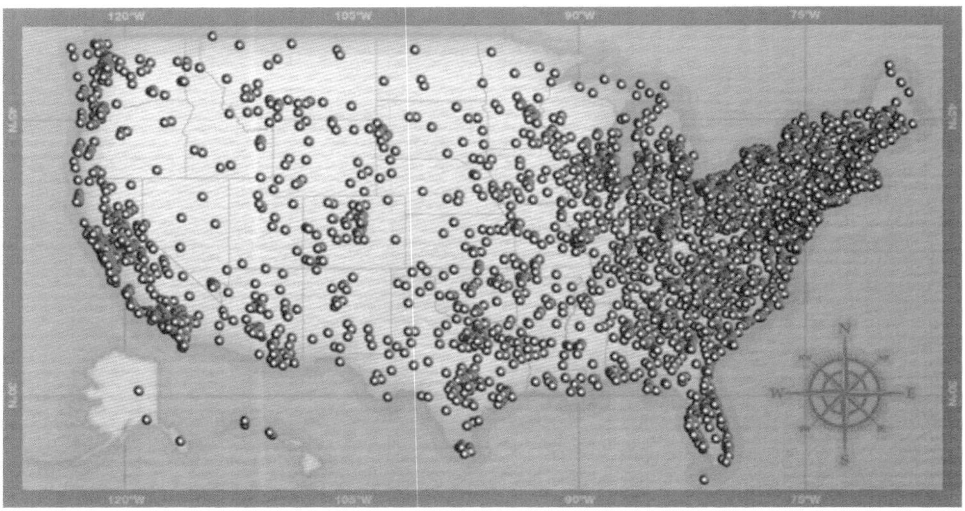